Pray Deep
for Advent

Kathryn Shirey

Copyright ©2015 Kathryn P. Shirey
Published by San Marco Publications
Frisco, TX

All Scripture quotations, unless otherwise indicated, are taken from the Holy Bible, New International Version®, NIV®. Copyright ©1973, 1978, 1984, 2011 by Biblica, Inc.™ Used by permission of Zondervan. All rights reserved worldwide. www.zondervan.com The "NIV" and "New International Version" are trademarks registered in the United States Patent and Trademark Office by Biblica, Inc.™

All Rights Reserved.
No part of this book may be reproduced or transmitted in any form or by any means including but not limited to information storage and retrieval systems, electronic, mechanical, photocopy, recording, etc. without written permission from the copyright holder, with exception of the prayers from the Book of Common Prayer which are not copyrighted.

ISBN: 978-0-9967318-2-9

First printing, October 2015

Almighty God, you have poured upon us the new light of your incarnate Word: Grant that this light, enkindled in our hearts, may shine forth in our lives; through Jesus Christ our Lord, who lives and reigns with you, in the unity of the Holy Spirit, one God, now and for ever. Amen.

*(A Collect for the First Sunday after Christmas Day, page 213,
The Book of Common Prayer)*

What is Advent?

Advent means "coming" and is a season in the church calendar of waiting with anticipation and expectation for the coming of Christ. During Advent, we remember God's faithfulness in the past and His prophecy over thousands of years of the birth of Jesus. We remember the coming of Jesus that first Christmas and what a gift God gave to us in sending His only son. We look expectantly toward the future coming of Jesus.

Advent is more than a countdown to Christmas, more than a few weeks to listen to Christmas songs on the radio, more than a reminder to finish your Christmas shopping. Rather it should be a time of preparing your heart for Jesus and finding the hope in our waiting.

Many churches and devotionals will focus on different themes each week during Advent. Traditionally, four candles are lit - one each week - as you progress through the season.

This journal will focus on the traditional themes of Hope, Peace, Joy, and Love. Each week, we'll look into different aspects of the week's theme:

- Remembering God's promises through Old Testament scripture.
- Reviewing Jesus' teaching and promises.
- Experiencing prayer through song.
- Exploring prayer through art.
- Stepping through the Christmas story and looking for these themes of hope, peace, joy and love.
- Examining our lives to see how we're living out these gifts from God and how we can share them with others.

This prayer journal is intended to enhance your advent season, bringing a greater focus on prayer and helping you find more hope, peace, joy, and love amid the hustle and bustle of this season.

How To Use This Journal

Advent begins on the fourth Sunday before Christmas. Depending on the calendar, the fourth Sunday could be a full week before Christmas or it could be Christmas Eve.

This prayer journal is designed to be used in any year, no matter how many days are in a particular Advent season. There are guided prayers for each day of four weeks, so you can use whichever ones are appropriate.

Plan to devote 20-30 minutes a day to prayer, if possible. The instructions on each day will guide you through that day's prayer.

Each day includes lined pages if you want to journal your prayer, your experience with that day's prayer, or how you hear God responding. You also have a blank page for extra notes, prayer doodles or anything else that comes to mind as you pray.

Use this time in prayer to focus on expectation and waiting for Jesus to come again. Ground yourself in the real meaning of the season and let this focus bring calm and purpose to all the Christmas preparations surrounding you.

Week 1: Hope
Sunday

Psalm 25:1-9

In you, Lord my God,
    I put my trust.
I trust in you;
    do not let me be put to shame,
    nor let my enemies triumph over me.
No one who hopes in you
    will ever be put to shame,
but shame will come on those
    who are treacherous without cause.
Show me your ways, Lord,
    teach me your paths.
Guide me in your truth and teach me,
    for you are God my Savior,
    and my hope is in you all day long.
Remember, Lord, your great mercy and love,
    for they are from of old.
Do not remember the sins of my youth
    and my rebellious ways;
according to your love remember me,
    for you, Lord, are good.
Good and upright is the Lord,
    therefore he instructs sinners in his ways.
He guides the humble in what is right
    and teaches them his way.

This week we'll focus on HOPE: the hope we have, the hope of more still yet to come.

As we walk through this season of waiting and expectation, where do you have hope? In this world of darkness, when it seems God is silent in our suffering, how do you stay rooted in hope? How can you have more hope in the promises of God through His son Jesus Christ?

Guide for Praying Deep Today:

Read Psalm 25 again. Linger over the words. Note which verses stand out to you and capture your heart. Circle or underline those words on the previous page.

Write out a prayer from the words in Psalm 25. Let God's words in this Psalm guide your prayer for the start of this Advent season and how you need to prepare your heart for Jesus. Pray for hope in the waiting and how you want your hope to grow in this Advent season.

Almighty God, give us grace to cast away the works of darkness, and put on the armor of light, now in the time of this mortal life in which your Son Jesus Christ came to visit us in great humility; that in the last day, when he shall come again in his glorious majesty to judge both the living and the dead, we may rise to the life immortal; through him who lives and reigns with you and the Holy Spirit, one God, now and for ever. Amen.

(A Collect for the First Sunday of Advent, page 211, The Book of Common Prayer)

Prayer Doodles / Notes / Sketches:

Prayer Doodles / Notes / Sketches:

Week 1: Hope
Monday

Guide for Praying Deep Today:

Read through the words of the hymn, "Come, Thou Long Expected Jesus", focusing on what the words mean for a people longing and hoping for the day Jesus makes all things new.

Say the words aloud. Underline the words that speak to you.

Pray through this hymn for your long expected Jesus and the hope you have in him, the hope you want to have in him.

Come, Thou Long Expected Jesus
Words: Charles Wesley, 1744   Public Domain

Come, thou long expected Jesus,
born to set thy people free;
from our fears and sins release us,
let us find our rest in thee.
Israel's strength and consolation,
hope of all the earth thou art;
dear desire of every nation,
joy of every longing heart.

Born thy people to deliver,
born a child and yet a King,
born to reign in us forever,
now thy gracious kingdom bring.
By thine own eternal spirit
rule in all our hearts alone;
by thine all sufficient merit,
raise us to thy glorious throne.

Prayer Doodles / Notes / Sketches:

> *Hope is being able to see that there is light despite all of the darkness.*
>
> *Desmond Tutu*

Week 1: Hope
Tuesday

Guide for Praying Deep Today:

Spend some time with Isaiah 9:2, reflecting on its message of hope. The Israelites had rebelled against God and were left in the darkness of God's silence for 400 years. Yet God foretold the coming of the great light of His son, giving the people hope in their waiting.

> **Isaiah 9:2**
>
> The people walking in darkness
>   have seen a great light;
> on those living in the land of deep darkness
>   a light has dawned.

Read the verse slowly, several times, listening with the "ear of your heart." Turn the words over and over in your mind, letting them soak deep into your soul.

Reflect on the words, attentive to the word or phrase that spoke the most to you.

Respond to that word or phrase by offering it up in prayer.

Rest in God. Sit in silence and listen for how God speaks to you through that word or phrase. Don't rush this part. See if you can spend 5-10 minutes in the silence and give God a chance to speak.

Remember how this verse spoke to you by journaling your experience, your prayer, and God's response on the following pages.

Prayer Doodles / Notes / Sketches:

> *Darkness cannot drive out darkness;
> only light can do that.
> Hate cannot drive out hate;
> only love can do that.*
>
> *Martin Luther King, Jr.*

Week 1: Hope
Wednesday

Guide for Praying Deep Today:

Grab your markers, pens, crayons, or colored pencils for today's prayer.

Reflect on the hope we have in our waiting. This Advent season reminds us we're still waiting for Jesus to return in glory to take us to our promised land. We live in a world of darkness today, yet Jesus is the great light who will eradicate all the dark.

Today we're going to pray through art. Mandalas are prayer circles. The circle is your sacred prayer space. You can color pictures or patterns in your circle, write words, doodle, or whatever the Spirit leads you to. You can also color or doodle outside the lines of the circle.

Some thoughts to get you started:

- What does this message of hope mean to you?
- Where do you need more hope in your life?
- What words from this week's scripture or hymn captured your heart?
- Who in your life needs prayers for hope?

Don't worry about result of your drawing. This is about the process of coloring or doodling and letting your mind wander through the thoughts God places on your heart. This is a time to spend in prayer, so relax into the process.

A lined page is provided if you choose to journal your experience or how you hear God responding.

Week 1: Hope
Thursday

Luke 1:26-38, 46-55

In the sixth month of Elizabeth's pregnancy, God sent the angel Gabriel to Nazareth, a town in Galilee, to a virgin pledged to be married to a man named Joseph, a descendant of David. The virgin's name was Mary. The angel went to her and said, "Greetings, you who are highly favored! The Lord is with you."

Mary was greatly troubled at his words and wondered what kind of greeting this might be. But the angel said to her, "Do not be afraid, Mary; you have found favor with God. You will conceive and give birth to a son, and you are to call him Jesus. He will be great and will be called the Son of the Most High. The Lord God will give him the throne of his father David, and he will reign over Jacob's descendants forever; his kingdom will never end."

"How will this be," Mary asked the angel, "since I am a virgin?"

The angel answered, "The Holy Spirit will come on you, and the power of the Most High will overshadow you. So the holy one to be born will be called the Son of God. Even Elizabeth your relative is going to have a child in her old age, and she who was said to be unable to conceive is in her sixth month. For no word from God will ever fail."

"I am the Lord's servant," Mary answered. "May your word to me be fulfilled." Then the angel left her.

And Mary said:
"My soul glorifies the Lord and my spirit rejoices in God my Savior,
for he has been mindful of the humble state of his servant.
From now on all generations will call me blessed,
for the Mighty One has done great things for me—holy is his name.
His mercy extends to those who fear him, from generation to generation.
He has performed mighty deeds with his arm;
   he has scattered those who are proud in their inmost thoughts.
He has brought down rulers from their thrones but has lifted up the humble.
He has filled the hungry with good things but has sent the rich away empty.
He has helped his servant Israel, remembering to be merciful
to Abraham and his descendants forever, just as he promised our ancestors."

GUIDE FOR PRAYING DEEP TODAY:

Read through the passage on the previous page a few times, until the story is familiar.

Next, close your eyes and place yourself in the story. Imagine being in Mary's place as the angel visits and delivers his message. Consider the social ramifications Mary would face for saying "yes."

Play the scene in your mind like a movie. Use all your senses to experience this moment and all its sounds, smells, and emotions.

Pay attention to the theme of hope through the scene.
- Where does hope enter, how does Mary experience hope?
- What might have caused her to lose hope and fall into despair? How did she overcome and hold onto hope?
- What hope do you take away from this story and how are you encouraged in this season of waiting and expectation?

Close with prayer, speaking your heart to Jesus.

Prayer Doodles / Notes / Sketches:

Week 1: Hope
Friday

Guide for Praying Deep Today:

Today, pray a version of the Examen as you reflect over this week. Start with a deep breath and relax into your prayers. **Ask for God's presence in your prayer time. Ask the Holy Spirit to open your eyes so you can see more clearly.**

Replay the week in your mind. Imagine you are reviewing with Jesus your actions and conversations, all that you did and all that you didn't do. Use the prompts below to guide your prayers.

Where this week have you experienced the hope we have in Jesus? Were there any times you felt distant from that hope? Were you able to share your hope with anyone else? **Ask God to show you how to fill your heart with hope.**

What gifts from God did you recognize in your week? Where has God blessed you? **Thank God for the gifts He lavishes us upon us.**

In this season of waiting and preparation for Jesus to come, how have you prepared your heart for Jesus? When this week have you felt God's presence most closely? How has that helped you experience hope in Jesus? **Ask God to prepare your heart to receive Jesus.**

Where have you struggled this week? Struggled with forgiveness, struggled to feel God's presence, struggled to find hope? **Ask God for forgiveness for anything holding your heart back from fully being present for Him. Ask God to open your heart and guide you in His paths.**

Ask God to go with you through the next week and guide your steps, preparing your heart for the coming of Jesus.

Prayer Doodles / Notes / Sketches:

> *Do not for a moment suppose that you must make yourself better, or prepare your heart for a worthy reception of Christ, but come at once - come as you are.*
>
> *Archibald Alexander*

Week 1: HOPE
Saturday

Guide for Praying Deep Today:

The Gift of Hope

Hope is a gift we've been given by God. The hope that even in the darkness, there will be light. Hope that even when we don't feel God's presence, He is there by our side. Hope that even when life's storms are swirling around us, we can find hope in God. Hope that there is forgiveness and grace in Jesus for all our sins and failures. Hope that Jesus will come back and lead us to God's kingdom.

Spend time today writing God a letter about the gift of hope. Use the prompts below to guide your prayers.

- How is hope a gift you've received from God?
- Pray to receive the gift of hope.
- Pray to bring Jesus the gift of a heart filled with hope.
- How can you share that gift of hope with others?
- Pray to share that gift of hope with others. Pray for specific people with whom you'd like to share the gift of hope in Jesus.

Prayer Doodles / Notes / Sketches:

> *Hope -- Hope in the face of difficulty. Hope in the face of uncertainty. The audacity of hope! In the end, that is God's greatest gift to us, the bedrock of this nation. A belief in things not seen. A belief that there are better days ahead.*
>
> *Barack Obama, speech, 2004 DNC Convention*

Week 2: PEACE
Sunday

This week we'll focus on PEACE: The peace that Jesus ushers into the world, the peace he will lead us to when he returns in glory, and the peace of knowing God has a bigger plan for this world.

The prophecies about Jesus in Isaiah were written more than 700 years before Jesus was born. Realizing just how vast God's vision and plans are can be steadying when our world today is in turmoil. Remember that God is at work both in your daily, personal world, but also on a scale beyond our comprehension. Hold onto the peace that He is greater than anything you may be facing.

Isaiah 9:6-7

For to us a child is born,
    to us a son is given,
        and the government will be on his shoulders
And he will be called
    Wonderful Counselor, Mighty God,
    Everlasting Father, Prince of Peace.
Of the greatness of his government and peace
    there will be no end.
He will reign on David's throne
    and over his kingdom,
establishing and upholding it
    with justice and righteousness
    from that time on and forever.
The zeal of the Lord Almighty
    will accomplish this.

GUIDE FOR PRAYING DEEP TODAY:

Read Isaiah 9:6-7 again. Linger over the words.

Note which verses stand out to you and capture your heart. Circle or underline those words on the previous page.

Write out a prayer from the words in Isaiah 9:6-7.

- Pray for peace as you prepare your heart for the coming of Jesus.
- Pray for peace knowing God is in charge and has bigger, deeper, wider plans than we can fathom.
- Pray for finding God's peace in the midst of our turbulent world.
- Pray for peace on earth this Christmas.

> Merciful God, who sent your messengers the prophets to preach repentance and prepare the way for our salvation: Give us grace to heed the warnings and forsake our sins, that we may greet with joy the coming of Jesus Christ our Redeemer; who lives and reigns with you and the Holy Spirit, one God, now and for ever. Amen.
>
> *(A Collect for the Second Sunday of Advent, page 211, The Book of Common Prayer)*

Prayer Doodles / Notes / Sketches:

Prayer Doodles / Notes / Sketches:

Week 2: PEACE
Monday

Guide for Praying Deep Today:

Read through the words of the hymn below, focusing on how the promise of Jesus can bring you peace. Underline the words that speak to you.

Pray through this hymn for "O Come, O Come, Immanuel," to come into your life and bring peace. Pray for peace in the wait, peace through the turmoil of our world, and peace in the world to come.

O Come, O Come, Immanuel
Text: Latin, 12th Century   Public Domain

O come, O come, Immanuel,
and ransom captive Israel
that mourns in lonely exile here
until the Son of God appear.

O come, O Wisdom from on high,
who ordered all things mightily;
to us the path of knowledge show
and teach us in its ways to go.

O come, O come, great Lord of might,
who to your tribes on Sinai's height
in ancient times did give the law
in cloud and majesty and awe.

O come, O Branch of Jesse's stem,
unto your own and rescue them!
From depths of hell your people save,
and give them victory o'er the grave.

O come, O Key of David, come
and open wide our heavenly home.
Make safe for us the heavenward road
and bar the way to death's abode.

O come, O Bright and Morning Star,
and bring us comfort from afar!
Dispel the shadows of the night
and turn our darkness into light.

O come, O King of nations, bind
in one the hearts of all mankind.
Bid all our sad divisions cease
and be yourself our King of Peace.

Rejoice! Rejoice! Immanuel
shall come to you, O Israel.

Prayer Doodles / Notes / Sketches:

> *God cannot give us a happiness and peace apart from Himself, because it is not there. There is no such thing.*
>
> *C. S. Lewis*

Week 2: Peace
Tuesday

Guide for Praying Deep Today:

Spend some time with John 14:27, reflecting on its message of peace.

John 14:27

"Peace I leave with you; my peace I give you. I do not give to you as the world gives. Do not let your hearts be troubled and do not be afraid."

Read the verse slowly, several times, listening with the "ear of your heart." Turn the words over and over in your mind, letting them soak deep into your soul.

Reflect on the words, attentive to the word or phrase that spoke the most to you.

Respond to that word or phrase by offering it up in prayer.

Rest in God. Sit in silence and listen for how God speaks to you through that word or phrase. Don't rush this part. See if you can spend 5-10 minutes in the silence and give God a chance to speak.

Remember how this verse spoke to you by journaling your experience, your prayer, and God's response on the following pages.

Prayer Doodles / Notes / Sketches:

> *If God be our God, He will give us peace in trouble. When there is a storm without, He will make peace within. The world can create trouble in peace, but God can create peace in trouble.*
>
> *Thomas Watson*

Week 2: Peace Wednesday

Guide for Praying Deep Today:

Grab your markers, pens, crayons, or colored pencils for today's prayer.

Reflect on the peace God gives us, even amidst the turmoil of our world., and the peace He promises to lead us to when Jesus comes again. How can we claim Jesus' gift of his peace in our lives and how can we share that gift with others?

Today we're going to pray through art. Mandalas are prayer circles. The circle is your sacred prayer space. You can color pictures or patterns in your circle, write words, doodle, or whatever the Spirit leads you to. You can also color or doodle outside the lines of the circle.

Some thoughts to get you started:

- What does this message of peace mean to you?
- Where do you need more peace in your life?
- What words from this week's scripture or hymn captured your heart?
- Who in your life needs prayers for peace?

Don't worry about result of your drawing. This is about the process of coloring or doodling and letting your mind wander through the thoughts God places on your heart. This is a time to spend in prayer, so relax into the process.

A lined page is provided if you choose to journal your experience or how you hear God responding.

Week 2: PEACE
Thursday

Luke 2:1-20

In those days Caesar Augustus issued a decree that a census should be taken of the entire Roman world. (This was the first census that took place while Quirinius was governor of Syria.) And everyone went to their own town to register.

So Joseph also went up from the town of Nazareth in Galilee to Judea, to Bethlehem the town of David, because he belonged to the house and line of David. He went there to register with Mary, who was pledged to be married to him and was expecting a child. While they were there, the time came for the baby to be born, and she gave birth to her firstborn, a son. She wrapped him in cloths and placed him in a manger, because there was no guest room available for them.

And there were shepherds living out in the fields nearby, keeping watch over their flocks at night. An angel of the Lord appeared to them, and the glory of the Lord shone around them, and they were terrified. But the angel said to them, "Do not be afraid. I bring you good news that will cause great joy for all the people. Today in the town of David a Savior has been born to you; he is the Messiah, the Lord. This will be a sign to you: You will find a baby wrapped in cloths and lying in a manger."

Suddenly a great company of the heavenly host appeared with the angel, praising God and saying,

"Glory to God in the highest heaven,
   and on earth peace to those on whom his favor rests."

When the angels had left them and gone into heaven, the shepherds said to one another, "Let's go to Bethlehem and see this thing that has happened, which the Lord has told us about."

So they hurried off and found Mary and Joseph, and the baby, who was lying in the manger. When they had seen him, they spread the word concerning what had been told them about this child, and all who heard it were amazed at what the shepherds said to them. But Mary treasured up all these things and pondered them in her heart. The shepherds returned, glorifying and praising God for all the things they had heard and seen, which were just as they had been told.

Guide for Praying Deep Today:

Read through the passage on the previous page a few times, until the story is familiar.

Next, close your eyes and place yourself in the story. Imagine being there in Bethlehem that night. Play the scene in your mind like a movie. Be in the stable with Mary and Joseph for the birth of Jesus. Keep watch with the shepherds and experience the angels' appearance.

Use all your senses to experience this moment and all its sounds, smells, and emotions.

Pay attention to the theme of peace through the scene.
- Where do you feel peace in the story?
- What parts of the story could bring fear instead of peace, and why does peace overcome?

Close with prayer, speaking your heart to Jesus.

Prayer Doodles / Notes / Sketches:

Week 2: Peace
Friday

Guide for Praying Deep Today:

Today, pray a version of the Examen as you reflect over this week. Start with a deep breath and relax into your prayers. **Ask for God's presence in your prayer time. Ask the Holy Spirit to open your eyes so you can see more clearly.**

Replay the week in your mind. Imagine you are reviewing with Jesus your actions and conversations, all that you did and all that you didn't do. Use the prompts below to guide your prayers.

Where this week have you experienced the peace we have through Jesus? Were there any times you felt distant from His peace? Were you able to share your peace through Jesus with anyone else? **Ask God to show you how to fill your heart with peace.**

What gifts from God did you recognize in your week? Where has God blessed you? **Thank God for the gifts He lavishes us upon us.**

When this week have you felt God's presence most closely? How has that helped you experience peace in Jesus? **Ask God to prepare your heart to receive peace through Jesus.**

Where have you struggled this week? Struggled with forgiveness, struggled to feel God's presence, struggled to feel at peace? **Ask God for forgiveness for anything holding your heart back from fully being present for Him. Ask God to open your heart and guide you in His paths.**

Ask God to go with you through the next week and guide your steps, preparing your heart for the coming of Jesus.

Prayer Doodles / Notes / Sketches:

> *Peace comes when there is no cloud between us and God. Peace is the consequence of forgiveness, God's removal of that which obscures His face and so breaks union with Him.*
>
> *Charles H. Brent*

Week 2: PEACE
Saturday

Guide for Praying Deep Today:

The Gift of Peace

Jesus gave us his gift of peace, his peace. His peace is an inner peace we can have even when the world around us is anything but peaceful. His is a peace in our hearts that comes from trusting God with our lives and our futures. Peace comes when we know God loves us and has a plan for us.

Spend time today writing God a letter about the gift of peace. Use the prompts below to guide your prayers.

- How is peace a gift you've received from God? Have you experienced His peace even through an uncertain and difficult time?
- Pray to receive the gift of peace.
- Pray to bring Jesus the gift of a heart filled with peace.
- How can you share that gift of peace with others?
- Pray to share that gift of peace with others. Pray for specific people with whom you'd like to share the gift of peace in Jesus.

Prayer Doodles / Notes / Sketches:

> God has given us two hands, one to receive with and the other to give with.
>
> Billy Graham

Week 3: Joy
Sunday

Zephaniah 3:14-20

Sing, Daughter Zion;
   shout aloud, Israel!
Be glad and rejoice with all your heart,
   Daughter Jerusalem!
The Lord has taken away your punishment,
   he has turned back your enemy.
The Lord, the King of Israel, is with you;
   never again will you fear any harm.
On that day
   they will say to Jerusalem,
"Do not fear, Zion;
   do not let your hands hang limp.
The Lord your God is with you,
   the Mighty Warrior who saves.
He will take great delight in you;
   in his love he will no longer rebuke you,
   but will rejoice over you with singing."
"I will remove from you
   all who mourn over the loss of your appointed festivals,
   which is a burden and reproach for you.
At that time I will deal
   with all who oppressed you.
I will rescue the lame;
   I will gather the exiles.
I will give them praise and honor
   in every land where they have suffered shame.
At that time I will gather you;
   at that time I will bring you home.
I will give you honor and praise
   among all the peoples of the earth
when I restore your fortunes
   before your very eyes,"
says the Lord.

Guide for Praying Deep Today:

This week we'll focus on JOY: The joy we have through Jesus, the ability for our hearts to rejoice, even when times are troubling. Joy that comes from anticipation of the promises of God.

Read Zephaniah 3:14-20 again. Linger over the words. Note which verses stand out to you and capture your heart. Circle or underline those words on the previous page.

Write out a prayer from the words in Zephaniah 3:14-20.

- Pray for joy as you prepare your heart for the coming of Jesus.
- Pray for joy and rejoicing to fill your heart, even amidst the trials of your life.
- Pray for joy in the Lord to take the place of worry and anxiety.
- Pray for your ability to share your joy with others and be a light in this world.

> Stir up your power, O Lord, and with great might come among us; and, because we are sorely hindered by our sins, let your bountiful grace and mercy speedily help and deliver us; through Jesus Christ our Lord, to whom, with you and the Holy Spirit, be honor and glory, now and for ever. Amen.
>
> *(A Collect for the Third Sunday of Advent, page 212, The Book of Common Prayer)*

Prayer Doodles / Notes / Sketches:

Prayer Doodles / Notes / Sketches:

Week 3: Joy
Monday

Guide for Praying Deep Today:

Read through the words of the hymn "Love Divine, All Loves Excelling" below, focusing on how Jesus can fill your heart with joy. Underline the words that speak to you.

Pray through this hymn for the joy of heaven to fill your life and leave you lost in wonder, love, and praise. Pray for others to receive the live-giving love of Jesus, fill of compassion, mercy, grace, and love.

Love Divine, All Loves Excelling
Text: Charles Wesley, 1747 Public Domain

Love divine, all loves excelling,
joy of heaven, to earth come down,
fix in us thy humble dwelling,
all thy faithful mercies crown.
Jesus, thou art all compassion,
pure, unbounded love thou art;
visit us with thy salvation;
enter every trembling heart.

Breathe, oh, breathe thy loving Spirit
into every troubled breast;
let us all in thee inherit;
let us find the promised rest.
Take away the love of sinning;
Alpha and Omega be;
end of faith, as its beginning,
set our hearts at liberty.

Come, Almighty, to deliver,
let us all thy life receive;
suddenly return, and never,
nevermore thy temples leave.
Thee we would be always blessing,
serve thee as thy hosts above,
pray and praise thee without ceasing,
glory in thy perfect love.

Finish, then, thy new creation;
pure and spotless let us be;
let us see thy great salvation
perfectly restored in thee:
changed from glory into glory,
till in heaven we take our place,
till we cast our crowns before thee,
lost in wonder, love and praise.

Prayer Doodles / Notes / Sketches:

Rejoice in the Lord always. I will say it again: Rejoice! Let your gentleness be evident to all. The Lord is near. Do not be anxious about anything, but in every situation, by prayer and petition, with thanksgiving, present your requests to God. And the peace of God, which transcends all understanding, will guard your hearts and your minds in Christ Jesus.

Philippians 4:4-7

Week 3: Joy
Tuesday

Isaiah 65:17-19

"See, I will create
 new heavens and a new earth.
The former things will not be remembered,
 nor will they come to mind.
But be glad and rejoice forever
 in what I will create,
for I will create Jerusalem to be a delight
 and its people a joy.
I will rejoice over Jerusalem
 and take delight in my people;
the sound of weeping and of crying
 will be heard in it no more.

Guide for Praying Deep Today:

Spend some time with Isaiah 65:17-19. Reflect on its message of joy.

Read the verse slowly, several times, listening with the "ear of your heart." Turn the words over and over in your mind, letting them soak deep into your soul.

Reflect on the words, attentive to the word or phrase that spoke the most to you.

Respond to that word or phrase by offering it up in prayer.

Rest in God. Sit in silence and listen for how God speaks to you through that word or phrase. Don't rush this part. See if you can spend 5-10 minutes in the silence and give God a chance to speak.

Remember how this verse spoke to you by journaling your experience, your prayer, and God's response on the following pages.

Prayer Doodles / Notes / Sketches:

Week 3: Joy
Wednesday

Guide for Praying Deep Today:

Grab your markers, pens, crayons, or colored pencils for today's prayer.

Reflect on the joy God gives us. Joy that can fill our hearts, even when we're filled with grief and sadness. Joy in the promise fulfilled in Jesus. Joy in the hope and mercy of Jesus. The joy that cries out to be glad and rejoice in the Lord always.

Today we're going to pray through art. Mandalas are prayer circles. The circle is your sacred prayer space. You can color pictures or patterns in your circle, write words, doodle, or whatever the Spirit leads you to. You can also color or doodle outside the lines of the circle.

Some thoughts to get you started:

- What does this message of joy mean to you?
- Where do you need more joy in your life?
- What words from this week's scripture or hymn captured your heart?
- Who in your life needs prayers for joy?

Don't worry about result of your drawing. This is about the process of coloring or doodling and letting your mind wander through the thoughts God places on your heart. This is a time to spend in prayer, so relax into the process.

A lined page is provided if you choose to journal your experience or how you hear God responding.

Week 3: Joy
Thursday

Matthew 2:1-12

After Jesus was born in Bethlehem in Judea, during the time of King Herod, Magi from the east came to Jerusalem and asked, "Where is the one who has been born king of the Jews? We saw his star when it rose and have come to worship him."

When King Herod heard this he was disturbed, and all Jerusalem with him. When he had called together all the people's chief priests and teachers of the law, he asked them where the Messiah was to be born. "In Bethlehem in Judea," they replied, "for this is what the prophet has written:

"'But you, Bethlehem, in the land of Judah,
    are by no means least among the rulers of Judah;
for out of you will come a ruler
    who will shepherd my people Israel.'"

Then Herod called the Magi secretly and found out from them the exact time the star had appeared. He sent them to Bethlehem and said, "Go and search carefully for the child. As soon as you find him, report to me, so that I too may go and worship him."

After they had heard the king, they went on their way, and the star they had seen when it rose went ahead of them until it stopped over the place where the child was. When they saw the star, they were overjoyed. On coming to the house, they saw the child with his mother Mary, and they bowed down and worshiped him. Then they opened their treasures and presented him with gifts of gold, frankincense and myrrh. And having been warned in a dream not to go back to Herod, they returned to their country by another route.

Guide for Praying Deep Today:

Read through the passage on the previous page a few times, until the story is familiar.

Next, close your eyes and place yourself in the story. Imagine traveling with the Magi, seeking the newborn king. Play the scene in your mind like a movie.

Use all your senses to experience this moment and all its sounds, smells, and emotions.

Pay attention to the theme of joy through the scene.
- Where do you see joy in the story?
- What fills the Magi with such joy and worship, even though they aren't Israelites?
- What keeps Herod's heart from being joyful at the birth of Jesus?

Close with prayer, speaking your heart to Jesus.

Prayer Doodles / Notes / Sketches:

Week 3: Joy
Friday

Guide for Praying Deep Today:

Today, pray a version of the Examen as you reflect over this week. Start with a deep breath and relax into your prayers. **Ask for God's presence in your prayer time. Ask the Holy Spirit to open your eyes so you can see more clearly.**

Replay the week in your mind. Imagine you are reviewing with Jesus your actions and conversations, all that you did and all that you didn't do. Use the prompts below to guide your prayers.

Where this week have you experienced the joy we have through Jesus? Were there any times you felt distant from His joy? Were you able to share your joy through Jesus with anyone else? **Ask God to show you how to fill your heart with joy.**

What gifts from God did you recognize in your week? Where has God blessed you? **Thank God for the gifts He lavishes us upon us.**

In this season of waiting and preparation for Jesus to come, how have you prepared your heart for Jesus? When this week have you felt God's presence most closely? How has that helped you experience joy in Jesus? **Ask God to prepare your heart to receive the joy of Jesus.**

Where have you struggled this week? Struggled with forgiveness, struggled to feel God's presence, struggled to feel joy? **Ask God for forgiveness for anything holding back the joy in your heart. Ask God to open your heart and guide you in His paths.**

Ask God to go with you through the next week and guide your steps, preparing your heart for the coming of Jesus.

Prayer Doodles / Notes / Sketches:

> *Good news from heaven the angels bring,*
> *Glad tidings to the earth they sing:*
> *To us this day a child is given,*
> *To crown us with the joy of heaven.*
>
> *Martin Luther*

week 3: joy
saturday

Guide for Praying Deep Today:

The Gift of Joy

Jesus gave us his gift of joy, a joy that surpasses all understanding. Joy that fills our heart, even through our sadness and uncertainty. Joy that comes from believing in the promises of God.

Spend time today writing God a letter about the gift of joy. Use the prompts below to guide your prayers.

- How is joy a gift you've received from God? Have you experienced His joy even when your circumstances are difficult?
- Pray to receive the gift of joy.
- Pray to bring Jesus the gift of a heart filled with joy.
- How can you share that gift of joy with others?
- Pray to share that gift of joy with others. Pray for specific people with whom you'd like to share the gift of joy in Jesus.

Prayer Doodles / Notes / Sketches:

> *I believe that a trusting attitude and a patient attitude go hand in hand. You see, when you let go and learn to trust God, it releases joy in your life. And when you trust God, you're able to be more patient. Patience is not just about waiting for something... it's about how you wait, or your attitude while waiting.*
>
> *Joyce Meyer*

Week 4: Love
Sunday

Psalm 89:1-8

I will sing of the Lord's great love forever;
   with my mouth I will make your faithfulness known
   through all generations.
I will declare that your love stands firm forever,
   that you have established your faithfulness in heaven itself.
You said, "I have made a covenant with my chosen one,
   I have sworn to David my servant,
'I will establish your line forever
   and make your throne firm through all generations.'"
The heavens praise your wonders, Lord,
   your faithfulness too, in the assembly of the holy ones.
For who in the skies above can compare with the Lord?
   Who is like the Lord among the heavenly beings?
In the council of the holy ones God is greatly feared;
   he is more awesome than all who surround him.
Who is like you, Lord God Almighty?
   You, Lord, are mighty, and your faithfulness surrounds you.

Guide for Praying Deep Today:

This week we'll focus on LOVE: The great love our God has for us, the love He sent through Jesus, the love the we spread through this world because Christ first loved us.

Read Psalm 89:1-8 again. Linger over the words. Note which verses stand out to you and capture your heart. Circle or underline those words on the previous page.

Write out a prayer from the words in Psalm 89:1-8.

- Pray for love as you prepare your heart for Christmas.
- Pray for love to fill your heart, so you might sing of the Lord's great love forever.
- Pray for your ability to share the love you've found in Jesus with others.
- Pray for our world to be filled with love, for God's love to soften the hearts of all those hardened by this world.

> *Purify our conscience, Almighty God, by your daily visitation, that your Son Jesus Christ, at his coming, may find in us a mansion prepared for himself; who lives and reigns with you, in the unity of the Holy Spirit, one God, now and for ever. Amen.*
>
> *(A Collect for the Fourth Sunday of Advent, page 212, The Book of Common Prayer)*

Prayer Doodles / Notes / Sketches:

Prayer Doodles / Notes / Sketches:

Week 4: Love
Monday

Guide for Praying Deep Today:

Read through the words of the hymn "Of the Father's Love Begotten" below, focusing on how Jesus can fill your heart with love. Underline the words that speak to you.

Pray through this hymn for the love of God, fulfilled in the birth of Jesus, to create in you a voice that wants to shout jubilee and extol His praises evermore. Pray for others to know the love God pours out on His children.

Of the Father's Love Begotten
Text: Aurelius Clemens Prudentius Public Domain

Of the Father's love begotten
ere the worlds began to be,
he is Alpha and Omega —
he the source, the ending he,
of the things that are, that have been,
and that future years shall see
evermore and evermore.

O that birth forever blessed,
when a virgin, blest with grace,
by the Holy Ghost conceiving,
bore the Savior of our race;
and the babe, the world's Redeemer,
first revealed his sacred face,
evermore and evermore.

This is he whom seers in old time
chanted of with one accord,
whom the voices of the prophets
promised in their faithful word;
now he shines, the long-expected;
let creation praise its Lord
evermore and evermore.

Let the heights of heaven adore him;
angel hosts, his praises sing:
powers, dominions, bow before him
and extol our God and King;
let no tongue on earth be silent,
every voice in concert ring
evermore and evermore.

Christ, to you, with God the Father
and the Spirit, there shall be
hymn and chant and high thanksgiving
and the shout of jubilee:
honor, glory, and dominion
and eternal victory
evermore and evermore.

Prayer Doodles / Notes / Sketches:

> The Christian does not think God will love us because we are good, but that God will make us good because He loves us.
>
> C. S. Lewis

Week 4: Love
Tuesday

Guide for Praying Deep Today:

Spend some time with John 13:34-35. Reflect on its message of love.

John 13:34-35

"A new command I give you: Love one another. As I have loved you, so you must love one another. By this everyone will know you are my disciples, if you love one another."

Read the verse slowly, several times, listening with the "ear of your heart." Turn the words over and over in your mind, letting them soak deep into your soul.

Reflect on the words, attentive to the word or phrase that spoke the most to you.

Respond to that word or phrase by offering it up in prayer.

Rest in God. Sit in silence and listen for how God speaks to you through that word or phrase. Don't rush this part. See if you can spend 5-10 minutes in the silence and give God a chance to speak.

Remember how this verse spoke to you by journaling your experience, your prayer, and God's response on the following pages.

Prayer Doodles / Notes / Sketches:

But God, being rich in mercy, because of the great love with which he loved us, even when we were dead in our trespasses, made us alive together with Christ— by grace you have been saved.

Ephesians 2:4-5

Week 4: Love
Wednesday

Guide for Praying Deep Today:

Grab your markers, pens, crayons, or colored pencils for today's prayer.

Reflect on the love God gives us. The unconditional, grace-filled love of our Heavenly Father on His children. The love that never ends and pours out on us every day. The love that fills our hearts to overflowing, so we can freely pour out to others. The love so deep that God sent His only Son to die for our sins, so that we might be saved.

Today we're going to pray through art. Mandalas are prayer circles. The circle is your sacred prayer space. You can color pictures or patterns in your circle, write words, doodle, or whatever the Spirit leads you to. You can also color or doodle outside the lines of the circle.

Some thoughts to get you started:

- What does this message of love mean to you?
- How do you feel God's love in your life? Where do you need to feel His love more powerfully?
- What words from this week's scripture or hymn captured your heart?
- Who in your life needs prayers for love?

Don't worry about result of your drawing. This is about the process of coloring or doodling and letting your mind wander through the thoughts God places on your heart. This is a time to spend in prayer, so relax into the process.

A lined page is provided if you choose to journal your experience or how you hear God responding.

Week 4: Love
Thursday

Luke 2:22-40

When the time came for the purification rites required by the Law of Moses, Joseph and Mary took him to Jerusalem to present him to the Lord (as it is written in the Law of the Lord, "Every firstborn male is to be consecrated to the Lord"), and to offer a sacrifice in keeping with what is said in the Law of the Lord: "a pair of doves or two young pigeons."

Now there was a man in Jerusalem called Simeon, who was righteous and devout. He was waiting for the consolation of Israel, and the Holy Spirit was on him. It had been revealed to him by the Holy Spirit that he would not die before he had seen the Lord's Messiah. Moved by the Spirit, he went into the temple courts. When the parents brought in the child Jesus to do for him what the custom of the Law required, Simeon took him in his arms and praised God, saying:

"Sovereign Lord, as you have promised,
  you may now dismiss your servant in peace.
For my eyes have seen your salvation,
  which you have prepared in the sight of all nations:
a light for revelation to the Gentiles,
  and the glory of your people Israel."

The child's father and mother marveled at what was said about him. Then Simeon blessed them and said to Mary, his mother: "This child is destined to cause the falling and rising of many in Israel, and to be a sign that will be spoken against, so that the thoughts of many hearts will be revealed. And a sword will pierce your own soul too."

There was also a prophet, Anna, the daughter of Penuel, of the tribe of Asher. She was very old; she had lived with her husband seven years after her marriage, and then was a widow until she was eighty-four. She never left the temple but worshiped night and day, fasting and praying. Coming up to them at that very moment, she gave thanks to God and spoke about the child to all who were looking forward to the redemption of Jerusalem.

When Joseph and Mary had done everything required by the Law of the Lord, they returned to Galilee to their own town of Nazareth. And the child grew and became strong; he was filled with wisdom, and the grace of God was on him.

Guide for Praying Deep Today:

Read through the passage on the previous page a few times, until the story is familiar.

Next, close your eyes and place yourself in the story. Imagine being in the temple courts this day when Simeon and Anna met the baby Jesus. Stand in their presence and experience this moment up close. Use each of your senses to experience this moment and all its sounds, smells, and emotions.

Pay attention to the theme of love through the scene.
- Where do you see God's love in the story?
- How is Simeon's heart filled with God's love in his waiting and in the fulfillment of God's promise?
- How is Mary filled with love, even through Simeon's prediction of heartache to come?
- What hope do you take away from this scene?

Close with prayer, speaking your heart to Jesus.

Prayer Doodles / Notes / Sketches:

week 4: LOVE
Friday

GUIDE FOR PRAYING DEEP TODAY:

Today, pray a version of the Examen as you reflect over this week. Start with a deep breath and relax into your prayers. **Ask for God's presence in your prayer time. Ask the Holy Spirit to open your eyes so you can see more clearly.**

Replay the week in your mind. Imagine you are reviewing with Jesus your actions and conversations, all that you did and all that you didn't do. Use the prompts below to guide your prayers.

Where this week have you experienced the love of God? Were there any times you felt distant from His love? Were you able to share God's love with anyone else? **Ask God to show you how to fill your heart with His love.**

What gifts from God did you recognize in your week? Where has God blessed you? **Thank God for the gifts He lavishes us upon us.**

When this week have you felt God's presence most closely? How has that helped you experience God's love? **Ask God to prepare your heart to receive His gift of love through Jesus.**

Where have you struggled this week? Struggled with forgiveness, struggled to feel God's presence, struggled to feel love? **Ask God for forgiveness for anything blocking His love to permeate your heart. Ask Him to fill your heart with His love and guide you in His paths.**

Ask God to go with you through the next week and guide your steps, preparing your heart for the coming of Jesus.

Prayer Doodles / Notes / Sketches:

> *Though we are incomplete, God loves us completely. Though we are imperfect, He loves us perfectly. Though we may feel lost and without compass, God's love encompasses us completely. ... He loves every one of us, even those who are flawed, rejected, awkward, sorrowful, or broken.*
>
> *Dieter F. Uchtdorf*

Week 4: Love
Saturday

Guide for Praying Deep Today:

The Gift of Love

God lavishes the gift of His love upon us, His children. He loves us so much that He sent Jesus to earth to live as one of us, to humble Himself as a baby to experience the human condition, and to die on the cross to save us. He loves you even when you don't feel lovable. He loves you deeply, unconditionally, and longs for you to accept His love.

Spend time today writing God a letter about the gift of love. Use the prompts below to guide your prayers.

- How is love a gift you've received from God? Have you experienced His love even when you didn't expect it or feel deserving of His love?
- What keeps you from fully receiving and accepting the gift of His unconditional, grace-filled love?
- Pray to receive the gift of love and ask God to remove any barriers keeping you from letting His love permeate your heart and soul.
- Pray to bring Jesus the gift of a heart filled with love.
- How can you share that gift of God's love with others?
- Pray to share that gift of God's love with others. Pray for specific people with whom you'd like to share the gift of God's love.

Prayer Doodles / Notes / Sketches:

> Christmas is the perfect time to celebrate the love of God and family and to create memories that will last forever. Jesus is God's perfect, indescribable gift. The amazing thing is that not only are we able to receive this gift, but we are able to share it with others on Christmas and every other day of the year.
>
> Joel Osteen

About Kathryn

Kathryn Shirey is a writer, a mom, and a fellow traveler on this journey of faith. Kathryn had something awesome happen when she asked God for guidance on where He wanted her to serve. He didn't answer as she expected, but that sent her on a journey of discovery.

She's not sure where God's taking her or what it will mean to "go to work for God", but she is committed to finding out!

Kathryn writes about prayer, growing closer to God, and God's vision for our lives on her blog, Finding Hope.

www.kathrynshirey.com

Connect with Kathryn online:

- Blog: www.kathrynshirey.com
- Facebook: www.facebook.com/FindingHopeKathryn
- Twitter: @KathrynPShirey
- Pinterest: www.pinterest.com/kpshirey

The "Pray Deep" Journals

The Pray Deep journal series is about igniting passion in your prayer life and forging a deeper relationship with God. Unlock the power and potential of prayer in your life by finding your best methods for prayer! Use the Pray Deep guided prayer journals to explore the different prayer methods and use this varied approach to prayer to pray through specific themes. Collect them all today! Available where books are sold.

Pray Deep: Ignite Your Prayer Life in 21 Days

This guided prayer journal introduces you to nearly 20 different prayer methods and guides you through daily prayer focused on the very nature of prayer and its role in your life. These 21 days will ignite your passion for prayer and grow your relationship with God.

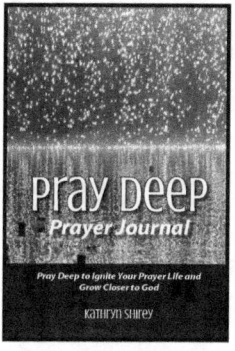

Pray Deep: Prayer Journal

This blank prayer journal is a perfect addition to your Prayer Closet, giving you lined and blank pages to record your prayers, key scriptures, and God's responses. It also includes a section to track specific prayer requests and includes guides for all the prayer methods introduced through "Pray Deep."

Pray Deep: Finding Stillness In Your Storms

A 21 day guided prayer journal exploring Psalm 46:10, "Be still and know that I am God." Through daily prayers, explore stillness with God, find Sabbath rest, and learn to hear and trust God in the middle of your life's storms.

www.ingramcontent.com/pod-product-compliance
Lightning Source LLC
Chambersburg PA
CBHW050541300426
44113CB00012B/2214